Unlocking the Door to Your Dream Home

A First-Time Buyer's Manual

By: Isaac Banahene Amoyaw

Table of Contents

Chapter 1

Understanding the Basics of Home Buying

The Benefits of Homeownership

Owning a home is a dream for many individuals. It provides stability, security, and the opportunity to create a space that reflects your personality and lifestyle. In this subchapter, we will explore the various benefits of homeownership, shedding light on why it is a wise investment for first-time homebuyers.

One of the significant advantages of homeownership is building equity. Unlike renting, where your monthly payments only benefit the landlord, each mortgage payment contributes to building equity in your property when you own a home. Over time, as property values increase, your house becomes an asset that can provide a substantial return on investment.

Furthermore, owning a home allows you to take advantage of tax benefits. In many countries, homeowners are eligible for tax deductions on mortgage interest, property taxes, and even specific home improvements. These deductions can significantly reduce your overall tax liability, providing additional financial relief and incentives to invest in homeownership.

Another advantage of owning a home is the freedom to make it your own. Unlike rental properties, where you may be restricted in making changes or improvements, homeownership empowers you to personalise your space according to your preferences. Whether painting the walls, renovating the kitchen, or creating a beautiful garden, you can transform your house into a home that reflects your style and taste.

Homeownership also offers stability and security for you and your family. When you own a home, you do not have to worry about sudden rent increases or the possibility of eviction. You have the assurance of a stable living situation, which is particularly important for those with children or individuals looking to settle down in a specific area for the long term.

Lastly, homeownership provides a sense of community and belonging. As a homeowner, you become part of a neighbourhood where you can build lasting relationships with your neighbours and actively contribute to the community. Homeowners often have a stronger sense of pride and engagement in their surroundings, fostering a sense of belonging and creating a supportive network.

In conclusion, the benefits of homeownership are numerous and extend beyond the financial aspect. From building equity and tax benefits to personalisation and stability, owning a home is an investment in your future and a step towards achieving your dreams. As a first-time homebuyer, understanding these advantages will help you make an informed decision and unlock the door to your dream home.

Assessing Your Financial Readiness

One of the most critical aspects of purchasing your dream home is ensuring that you are financially prepared for such a significant investment. As a first-time homebuyer, assessing your financial readiness before leaping into homeownership is essential. This subchapter will guide you through evaluating your financial situation, helping you determine if you are ready to embark on this exciting journey.

The first step in assessing your financial readiness is closely examining your current financial situation. This includes evaluating your income, expenses, and debt obligations. It is crucial to clearly understand your monthly cash flow and how much you can comfortably allocate towards a mortgage payment. Consider any potential changes in your income in the future, such as career advancements or starting a family, as these factors can impact your financial stability.

Next, it is essential to calculate your debt-to-income ratio (DTI). This ratio compares your monthly debt payments to your gross monthly income. Lenders typically prefer a DTI ratio of 36% or lower. If your ratio exceeds this threshold, it may be necessary to pay down some debt before pursuing homeownership.

Another vital aspect of assessing your financial readiness is examining your credit score. A good credit score can significantly impact your ability to secure a favourable mortgage rate. Please obtain a copy of your credit report and review it for errors or discrepancies. If your credit score is lower than desired, improve it by paying bills on time, reducing credit card balances, and avoiding new credit applications.

Additionally, consider the costs associated with homeownership beyond the mortgage payment. These expenses include property taxes, homeowner's insurance, maintenance, and repairs. An emergency fund is crucial to cover unexpected costs that may arise as a homeowner.

Lastly, consult with a mortgage lender or financial advisor to understand your borrowing capacity and the various mortgage options. They can help you determine the mortgage amount you qualify for, the down payment required, and the associated closing costs.

Assessing your financial readiness is crucial to achieving your dream of homeownership. By evaluating your income, expenses, debt obligations, credit score, and additional homeownership costs, you can ensure that you are financially prepared to take this significant step. Remember, being economically ready provides peace of mind and sets a solid foundation for a successful homeownership journey.

Setting Realistic Goals and Expectations

As a first-time home buyer, having dreams and aspirations for your future home is natural. However, setting realistic goals and expectations is crucial to ensure a successful and satisfying buying experience. This subchapter will explore the importance of setting achievable objectives and managing expectations to help you unlock the door to your dream home.

When setting goals, it's essential to consider your financial situation and limitations. Evaluate your budget, analyse your income, and determine the maximum amount you can comfortably afford for a home. This will help you narrow your search and focus on properties within your price range. Setting a realistic financial goal will prevent disappointment and unnecessary stress during buying.

Furthermore, aligning your goals with your needs and priorities is crucial. Consider your lifestyle, family size, and plans. Determine the number of bedrooms, bathrooms, and overall square footage required to accommodate your needs adequately. Identifying your non-negotiables will help you stay focused and make informed decisions.

While it's essential to have dreams, it's equally important to manage your expectations. Finding the perfect home may be challenging, especially within your budget. Be prepared to compromise on certain aspects and prioritise what truly matters. Remember, most houses will require some maintenance and improvements, so it's crucial to be realistic about the condition of the properties you come across.

Additionally, managing your expectations involves understanding the buying process itself. Educate yourself about the local real estate market, current trends, and the typical home purchase timeline. This knowledge will help you set realistic expectations regarding the availability of properties, negotiation strategies, and potential delays that may arise.

In conclusion, setting realistic goals and expectations is vital for first-time home buyers. By understanding your financial limitations, aligning your goals with your needs, and managing your expectations, you can embark on the home-buying journey confidently and clearly. Remember, finding the perfect home may take time and compromise, but with realistic goals, you will be well on your way to unlocking the door to your dream home.

Chapter 2

Exploring the Real Estate Market

Researching Local Neighbourhoods

One of the most crucial steps in buying your first home is researching local neighbourhoods. The neighbourhood you choose will significantly impact your daily life, so finding a community that aligns with your needs and preferences is essential. This subchapter will guide you through researching local neighbourhoods, helping you make an informed decision and find your dream home.

Firstly, start by identifying your priorities. Consider factors such as commute time, school proximity, healthcare facilities, recreational areas, and shopping centres. Think about the lifestyle you want to lead and the essential amenities for you and your family. This will help you narrow your search and focus on neighbourhoods that meet your criteria.

Next, gather information about the potential neighbourhoods you are interested in. Utilise online resources, such as real estate websites, neighbourhood review sites, and local government websites. These platforms provide valuable insights into crime rates, school ratings, property values, and other essential data. Additionally, join regional community forums or social media groups to connect with current residents and gather their firsthand experiences.

Visiting the neighbourhoods in person is crucial to get a feel for the area. Take a drive or walk around during different times of the day to observe the traffic, noise levels, and general ambience. Explore nearby parks, restaurants, and shops to gauge the community's vibrancy and availability of amenities.

Another valuable research tool is talking to locals. Strike up conversations with neighbours, shop owners, and community members to gather information about the neighbourhood's safety, community events, and potential concerns. Their experiences and insights can give you a deeper understanding of the area.

Additionally, consider working with a local real estate agent with in-depth knowledge of the neighbourhoods you are interested in. They can provide valuable guidance, answer your questions, and help you find the perfect home in a suitable area.

Remember, thorough research is vital to finding the right neighbourhood for your first home. By analysing your priorities, gathering information, visiting in person, and talking to locals, you'll have the knowledge needed to make an informed decision. Researching local neighbourhoods will ensure you unlock the door to your dream home in a community that suits your lifestyle and needs.

Evaluating Property Values

When buying your dream home, one of the most crucial steps is evaluating property values. As a first-time home buyer, it's essential to understand how to assess the value of a property to ensure you make a wise investment. In this chapter, we will explore the key factors to consider when evaluating property values, providing you with the knowledge and tools necessary to make an informed decision.

Firstly, one of the primary aspects to evaluate is the property's location. Location plays a vital role in determining the value of a home. Consider proximity to schools, healthcare facilities, shopping centres, and transportation options. A desirable location will enhance your quality of life and contribute to the property's future resale value.

Secondly, it's crucial to assess the condition and age of the property. A thorough inspection is essential to identify any potential issues or necessary repairs. Understanding the property's current situation will allow you to estimate maintenance costs and negotiate a fair price. Remember, older homes may have more potential maintenance needs, impacting the overall value.

Another critical factor to consider is the size and layout of the property. Determine whether the size meets your needs and whether the design fits your lifestyle. Additionally, consider the potential for expansion or renovation in the future, as this can significantly impact the property's value.

Furthermore, researching recent comparable sales in the area will provide insights into the property's market value. Look for similar properties in size, condition, and location to understand the property. Utilise online real estate platforms, consult with local agents, or attend open houses to gather information on recent sales.

Lastly, consider the economic factors that may affect property values in the future. Research the local economy, job market, and any upcoming developments or infrastructure projects that may impact property prices positively or negatively.

Evaluating property values is a critical step in the home-buying process. By considering location, property condition, size and layout, recent comparable sales, and economic factors, you will be equipped with the knowledge to make an informed decision. Remember, a thorough evaluation will help you find your dream home and ensure that you make an intelligent investment for your future.

Understanding Market Trends and Conditions

As a first-time home buyer, understanding market trends and conditions is one of the most crucial aspects to consider before embarking on your home-buying journey. These factors can significantly impact your decision-making process and ultimately determine the success of your investment. This subchapter will delve into the importance of staying informed about market trends and conditions and how to use this knowledge to your advantage.

Market trends refer to the patterns and movements observed in the real estate market over a specific period. By analysing these trends, you can gain valuable insights into the current state of the market, anticipate future changes, and make informed decisions. On the other hand, understanding market conditions involves assessing various factors influencing the real estate market, such as supply and demand, interest rates, employment rates, and economic indicators.

Awareness of market trends and conditions empowers you to make strategic choices when buying your dream home. For instance, during a buyer's market, where a surplus of homes is available for sale, you may have more negotiating power and find better deals. Conversely, in a seller's market, where demand exceeds supply, you may need to act quickly and be prepared to pay a premium for the property you desire. Understanding the current market conditions allows you to adjust your expectations and approach accordingly.

To stay informed about market trends, it is essential to research and analyse real estate data, consult with local experts, and follow reputable sources of information. Real estate websites, industry publications, and experienced agents can provide valuable insights into the local market. Additionally, attending open houses and networking with other home buyers can give you a sense of the current demand and competition.

Remember that market trends and conditions can fluctuate, so regularly updating your knowledge is crucial. By monitoring the market, you can identify emerging trends, such as changes in buyer preferences or shifts in the local economy, which may impact the value of your investment.

Understanding market trends and conditions is critical to successful home buying for first-time buyers. By equipping yourself with this knowledge, you can confidently navigate the market, make informed decisions, and unlock the door to your dream home.

Chapter 3

Budgeting for Your Dream Home

Determining Affordability and Mortgage Options

When purchasing your first home, it is essential to determine affordability and explore various mortgage options. This subchapter will guide you through understanding your financial capabilities and choosing the right mortgage for your dream home.

Before embarking on your home-buying journey, it is crucial to assess your financial situation. Start by evaluating your income, expenses, and savings. This will help you understand how much you can comfortably afford to spend on a monthly mortgage payment. Remember to consider other costs associated with homeownership, such as property taxes, insurance, and maintenance expenses.

Once you have determined your affordability, it is time to explore mortgage options. There are several types of mortgages available, and understanding them will enable you to make an informed decision.

1. Conventional Mortgage: This is the most common type of mortgage, often requiring a down payment of 20% or more. It offers competitive interest rates and flexible terms, making it a popular choice for first-time buyers with good credit.

2. FHA Mortgage: Insured by the Federal Housing Administration, this mortgage option allows buyers with a lower down payment (as low as 3. 5%) and a less-than-perfect credit score to qualify for a loan. It is an excellent option for those who may not meet the requirements of a conventional mortgage.

3. VA Loan: Available to eligible veterans and active-duty military personnel, a VA loan offers 100% financing with no down payment required. It also provides competitive interest rates and flexible terms.

4. USDA Loan: Designed for individuals purchasing homes in rural areas, a USDA

loan offers 100% financing and low interest rates. This mortgage option is excellent for those seeking affordable housing in rural communities.

5. Adjustable-Rate Mortgage (ARM): With an ARM, the interest rate fluctuates over time. Initially, it may be lower than a fixed-rate mortgage, making it attractive to buyers who plan to stay in their homes for a short period. However, it is crucial to understand the risks associated with potential interest rate hikes.

As a first-time homebuyer, it is crucial to research and compare different mortgage options to find the one that best suits your needs and financial situation. Consult a reputable mortgage lender who can guide you through the process and help you make an informed decision.

Remember, determining affordability and choosing the right mortgage is crucial to unlocking the door to your dream home. By understanding your financial capabilities and exploring various mortgage options, you will be well-prepared to embark on your exciting journey as a first-time homebuyer.

Saving for a Down Payment

One of the biggest hurdles for first-time home buyers is saving enough money for a down payment. It can seem daunting, but with careful planning and discipline, you can make your dream of homeownership a reality. This subchapter will explore practical strategies to help you save for a down payment.

1. Set a realistic savings goal: Determine how much you need to save for a down payment. Typically, lenders require a down payment of 20% of the home's purchase price. However, options are also available for lower down payments, such as FHA loans that require as little as 3. 5%. Consider your financial situation and set a realistic savings goal based on your desired home price.

2. Create a budget: Developing a budget is a crucial step in saving for a down payment. Evaluate your monthly income and expenses to identify where to cut back and save more. Consider reducing discretionary spending, such as eating out or entertainment, and redirect those funds towards your down payment savings.

3. Open a dedicated savings account: Establish a separate account for your down payment funds. This will help you track your progress and prevent dipping into those savings for other expenses. Consider setting up automatic paycheck or checking account transfers to ensure consistent savings.

4. Explore down payment assistance programs: Research down payment assistance programs available in your area. These programs, offered by government agencies or non-profit organisations, can provide financial assistance or grants to first-time home buyers. Check with your local housing authority or consult a real estate professional to learn more about these opportunities.

5. Increase your income: Consider ways to boost your income to accelerate your savings. Look for part-time or freelance opportunities, ask for a raise at work, or pursue additional certifications or education to enhance your job prospects. Every extra dollar you earn can make a significant difference in reaching your down payment goal.

6. Make sacrifices: Saving for a down payment may require sacrifices. Consider

downsizing your living situation, reducing monthly bills, or temporarily cutting non-essential expenses. Remember, these sacrifices are temporary and will be worth it when you unlock the door to your dream home.

By following these strategies and staying focused on your goal, you can save for a down payment and take a significant step toward becoming a homeowner. Remember, patience, discipline, and perseverance are critical, and the reward of owning your own home will be well worth the effort.

Budgeting for Closing Costs and Other Expenses

Congratulations! You have taken the first step towards homeownership by buying your dream home. As a first-time homebuyer, it is essential to understand the financial obligations that come with this exciting milestone. One crucial aspect to consider is budgeting for closing costs and other expenses. This subchapter will guide you through estimating and preparing for these additional financial responsibilities.

Closing costs refer to the fees and expenses associated with finalising the purchase of your home. While the exact amount varies depending on location and purchase price, it typically ranges from 2% to 5% of the home's value. These costs include appraisal fees, attorney fees, title insurance, and loan origination fees. It is crucial to factor these costs into your budget to ensure a smooth and stress-free closing process.

To budget for closing costs, start by researching and understanding the average closing costs in your area. This will give you a ballpark figure to work with. Next, assess your financial situation and determine how much you can comfortably allocate towards closing costs. Remember to consider your down payment, monthly mortgage payments, and other ongoing expenses when setting your budget.

In addition to closing costs, there are other expenses to consider when purchasing your first home. These include moving costs, home inspections, and potential repairs or renovations. It is vital to account for these expenses as they can quickly add up. Create a comprehensive list of all possible costs and prioritise them based on urgency and importance.

To ensure you are financially prepared, consider setting up a dedicated savings conclusion, budgeting for closing costs and other expenses is crucial for first-time homebuyers. By estimating and preparing for these financial obligations, you can ensure a smooth and stress-free home-buying process. Take the time to research average closing costs in your area, assess account for your home purchase. This will allow you to save consistently and track your progress toward your financial goals. Automating your savings can also help you stay on track and avoid the temptation to dip into your home-buying fund for other expenses.

Remember, being aware of these additional costs and budgeting for them will help you avoid any financial surprises and ensure a successful home-buying experience. By planning and making informed financial decisions, you will be well on your way to unlocking the door to your dream home.

In your financial situation, and create a comprehensive budget. By doing so, you will be well-prepared to make your homeownership dreams a reality.

Chapter 4

<hr>

Securing Financing for Your Home

Understanding Different Types of Mortgages

When purchasing your first home, understanding the different types of mortgages available is crucial. A mortgage is a loan specifically designed for homebuyers, allowing them to pay for their dream home over some time. In this subchapter, we will delve into the various types of mortgages and help you make an informed decision.

1. Fixed-Rate Mortgage: This is one of the most popular types of mortgages for first-time homebuyers. With a fixed-rate mortgage, the interest rate remains unchanged throughout the loan term, providing stability and predictability. This allows you to plan your budget effectively, knowing exactly how much you must pay each month.

2. Adjustable-Rate Mortgage (ARM): Unlike a fixed-rate mortgage, an adjustable-rate mortgage offers an interest rate that changes periodically. Typically, the initial interest rate is lower than that of a fixed-rate mortgage, making it an attractive option for those who plan to sell or refinance before the rate adjusts. However, it's essential to understand the terms and potential risks associated with an ARM.

3. Federal Housing Administration (FHA) Loan: Aimed at first-time homebuyers with lower credit scores or limited down payment funds, an FHA loan is insured by the Federal Housing Administration. This type of mortgage offers flexible qualification requirements and lower down payments, making homeownership more accessible for many.

4. Department of Veterans Affairs (VA) Loan: Available exclusively to veterans, active-duty military personnel, and their eligible spouses, the Department of Veterans Affairs guarantees VA loans. These loans often offer favourable terms, including low or zero down payment requirements, competitive interest rates, and no private mortgage insurance.

5. Jumbo Loan: A jumbo loan is a mortgage that exceeds the loan limits set by government-sponsored enterprises. This type of loan is typically used for high-value properties and requires a larger down payment and a strong credit score.

Understanding the different types of mortgages is crucial to finding the right one for your specific needs and financial situation. When deciding, it's essential to consider factors such as interest rates, loan terms, and eligibility requirements. Consulting with a mortgage advisor or lender can provide valuable guidance.

Remember, purchasing a home is a significant decision, and choosing the right mortgage is an essential part of the process. By understanding the different types of mortgages available, you can make an informed choice that aligns with your financial goals and aspirations.

Preparing and Organising Your Financial Documents

When purchasing your dream home, one of the most crucial steps is preparing and organising your financial documents. As a first-time homebuyer, you must have all your financial ducks in a row to ensure a smooth and stress-free buying process. This subchapter will guide you through the necessary steps to manage your finances.

The first thing you need to do is gather all your financial documents. This includes your bank statements, tax returns for the past two years, pay stubs, and any other proof of income. Lenders will want to see these documents to assess your financial stability and determine how much mortgage you can afford. Make sure to have digital and hard copies of these documents for easy access.

Next, it is crucial to organise your documents logically. Create separate folders for each type of document and label them clearly. This will make it easier to find specific information when needed. Consider creating a spreadsheet or using a budgeting app to track expenses and income. This will give you a clear picture of your financial health and help you make informed decisions.

As a first-time homebuyer, you may also need to gather additional documents specific to the home-buying process. These may include rental agreements, credit reports, and proof of assets. Stay organised by keeping these documents in a separate folder, easily accessible when required.

Once you have all your documents in order, it is time to review them carefully. Look for any discrepancies or errors that could affect your mortgage application. If you find any issues, address them immediately to avoid delays in the buying process.

Finally, consider consulting with a financial advisor or mortgage broker. They can guide you through the process and help you understand the financial documents better. They can also provide valuable advice on improving your financial profile if needed.

In conclusion, preparing and organising your financial documents is crucial for any first-time homebuyer. By gathering your records, you will be well-prepared to navigate the home-buying process smoothly by gathering and organising them, reviewing them carefully, and seeking professional advice. Remember, a little effort upfront can save you time and stress in the long run, bringing you one step closer to unlocking the door to your dream home.

Applying for a Mortgage and Getting Pre-approved

As a first-time home buyer, applying for a mortgage and getting pre-approved can seem daunting and overwhelming. However, it is an essential step towards unlocking the door to your dream home. This subchapter aims to guide you through the process, providing valuable insights and tips to help you confidently navigate this crucial stage.

Getting pre-approved for a mortgage is essential before you start house hunting. It lets you determine your budget and lets sellers know you are a serious buyer. First, gather all the necessary financial documents, such as pay stubs, tax returns, and bank statements. These documents will help lenders assess your financial situation and determine your eligibility for a mortgage.

Next, research different lenders and mortgage options to find the best fit for your needs. Compare interest rates, loan terms, and fees to make an informed decision. It's always a good idea to consult a mortgage broker who can provide expert advice and help you find the most suitable mortgage option.

When you're ready to apply, be prepared to provide detailed information about your employment, income, assets, and debts. This information will help lenders assess your financial stability and determine the amount of mortgage you can qualify for. It's crucial to be honest and accurate when providing this information to avoid any complications later in the process.

After submitting your application, the lender will review your information and conduct a credit check. This will help them assess your creditworthiness and determine the interest rate you qualify for. Maintaining a good credit score is essential to paying bills on time, reducing outstanding debts, and avoiding significant financial decisions during application.

You'll receive a pre-approval letter once you've been pre-approved for a mortgage. This letter will outline the amount you qualify for and any conditions attached to the approval. With this letter, you can confidently start house hunting within your budget.

In conclusion, you are applying for a mortgage and getting pre-approved is a crucial step to your dream of owning a home.

Gathering the necessary documents, researching lenders, and providing accurate information can increase your chances of a successful application. Getting pre-approved helps you determine your budget and shows sellers you are a serious buyer. Take the time to understand the process, consult with professionals, and make informed decisions to ensure a smooth and successful mortgage application.

Chapter 5

Navigating the Home Search
Process

Defining Your Home Preferences and Must-Haves

Defining your home preferences and must-haves is crucial when embarking on the exciting journey of buying your first home. This subchapter will guide you through identifying what you truly desire in your dream home, helping you make informed decisions and avoid costly mistakes.

Before you start browsing through listings or attending open houses, take the time to reflect on your lifestyle, needs, and long-term goals. Begin by considering the size of the home you require. Are you planning to start a family shortly? Do you need additional space for a home office or a guest room? Understanding your spatial needs will help narrow your search and prevent you from purchasing a home that may soon feel cramped.

Next, think about the location that suits your lifestyle. Consider proximity to work, schools, amenities, and public transportation. Do you prefer a quiet suburban neighbourhood or bustling city life? Evaluating the neighbourhood's safety, local services, and community atmosphere will ensure you find a location that aligns with your preferences.

When it comes to the features and amenities of your dream home, create a list of must-haves and nice-to-haves. Must-haves are non-negotiable features that you cannot compromise on. These could include the number of bedrooms and bathrooms, a backyard for your pets, or a spacious kitchen for your culinary adventures. Nice-to-haves, on the other hand, are desirable but not essential. These could include a swimming pool, a fireplace, or a dedicated home theatre room.

Remember to prioritise your must-haves and remain flexible on the nice-to-haves. Sometimes, you may find a home that lacks a few nice-to-haves but meets all your must-haves, making it an ideal choice. Additionally, consider the potential for future renovations or upgrades that can turn a good house into your dream home.

Lastly, it is essential to establish a budget for your home purchase. Take into account your income, savings, and other financial obligations. Consult with a mortgage professional to determine your borrowing capacity and get pre-approved for a loan. This will give you a clear understanding of your budget, allowing you to focus on homes within your price range.

Defining your home preferences and must-haves is a crucial step in the home-buying process. By understanding your needs, desires, and financial limitations, you can make informed decisions and find a home that truly reflects your dreams and aspirations. Remember, your dream home is out there waiting for you – all you need to do is define it.

Working with a Real Estate Agent

When buying your first home, the process can be overwhelming. It can feel daunting, from searching for properties to negotiating prices and navigating the legal paperwork. That's where a real estate agent comes in. Working with a professional can make the entire experience smoother and more enjoyable for first-time home buyers.

Real estate agents are housing market experts with the knowledge and experience to guide you through home-buying. They will listen to your needs and preferences and help you find properties that meet your criteria. With their expertise, they can save you time by narrowing your search to homes that are a good fit for you.

One of the most significant advantages of working with a real estate agent is their negotiation skills. They will act as your advocate when making an offer on a property. They will help you determine a fair price to offer and negotiate with the seller on your behalf. They aim to get you the best possible deal and protect your interests throughout the transaction.

Furthermore, a real estate agent can provide valuable insights and advice during home-buying. They can help you understand the local market trends, provide information about the neighbourhood and amenities, and answer any questions. Their expertise can help you make informed decisions and avoid potential pitfalls.

When selecting a real estate agent, finding someone who is trustworthy, responsive, and understands your needs is essential.

Look for an agent with experience working with first-time home buyers and a strong track record of successful transactions. You can ask for recommendations from friends or family, search for agents online, and read reviews from previous clients.

In conclusion, working with a real estate agent is highly recommended for first-time home buyers. Their expertise, negotiation skills, and guidance can make the home-buying process less stressful and more successful. So, don't hesitate to contact a professional and unlock the door to your dream home!

Attending Open Houses and Private Showings

Open houses and private showings are essential steps in the home-buying process. Not only do they allow you to explore potential dream homes, but they also provide valuable insights into the real estate market. Attending these events can be exciting and overwhelming as a first-time home buyer. This subchapter aims to guide you through the dos and don'ts of attending open houses and private showings, ensuring you make the most of these opportunities.

1.   Research and Plan Ahead: Before attending any open house or a private showing, conduct thorough research on the property and the neighbourhood it's located in. Familiarise yourself with the local market trends, schools, amenities, and transportation options. Plan your visit accordingly to ensure you have enough time to explore the area and ask pertinent questions.

2. Make a Checklist: Create a checklist of features essential to you in a home. This will help you stay focused and evaluate each property objectively. Take notes and pictures during your visit to help you remember each property's unique aspects.

3. Be Punctual and Professional: Arrive on time and dress appropriately when attending open houses or private showings. Being punctual shows respect for the real estate agent and allows you ample time to explore the property. Remember to be professional and polite when interacting with the agent or the seller.

4. Ask Relevant Questions: Prepare a list of questions for the agent or seller during the open house or private showing. Inquire about the property's history, any renovations or

repairs, and the reason for selling. Ask about the neighbourhood, amenities, and potential issues affecting the property's value.

5. Observe and Inspect: Pay attention to the property's condition, layout, and functionality. Take note of potential maintenance or repair issues, such as leaky faucets, cracks, or faulty wiring. Consider how the space will meet your needs and whether any modifications or improvements will be necessary.

6. Network and Gather Information: Engage with other attendees, real estate agents, and neighbours if available. Networking can provide valuable insights into the neighbourhood and potential developments affecting property values.

7. Follow-Up: If you're interested in a particular property, follow up with the agent or seller after the open house or private showing. Express your interest and inquire about the next steps in the buying process. This will show your seriousness as a buyer and may give you an advantage if there are multiple interested parties.

Attending open houses and private showings is an essential part of your journey to finding your dream home. By following these tips and being prepared, you can make the most of these opportunities and gain a deeper understanding of the real estate market. Remember to trust your instincts and take your time in finding the perfect home that meets your needs and aspirations.

Chapter 6

Making an Offer and Negotiating

Understanding the Offer Process

As a first-time homebuyer, making an offer on a house can be exciting and nerve-wracking. This subchapter aims to provide a comprehensive understanding of the offer process, helping you navigate this crucial step in purchasing your dream home.

Before making an offer, you must do your homework and thoroughly research the real estate market. By understanding the current market trends, you will be better equipped to make a competitive offer that stands out. Additionally, it is crucial to clearly understand your budget and what you can afford, as this will determine the offer amount.

Once you have found the perfect home, the next step is to submit a written offer to the seller or their real estate agent. This offer should include various elements such as the purchase price, the desired closing date, any contingencies (such as inspections or financing), and any additional terms or conditions you may want to include. It is essential to consult with your real estate agent or attorney when drafting the offer to ensure all legal aspects are covered.

After submitting your offer, the seller will review it and may choose to accept, reject, or make a counteroffer. Maintaining open communication with your real estate agent during this stage is essential, as they can help negotiate on your behalf and guide you through the process. Sometimes, the property may have multiple offers, leading to a bidding war. Your agent can advise you on navigating these situations and increase your chances of securing the home.

Once your offer has been accepted, staying on top of the timeline and following through with any agreed-upon contingencies is crucial. This may include conducting inspections, securing financing, and completing necessary paperwork. Your real estate agent will assist you in coordinating these tasks to ensure a smooth closing process.

Understanding the offer process is vital for first-time homebuyers to navigate the real estate market successfully. By conducting thorough research, working closely with a trusted real estate agent, and staying organised, you can confidently offer your dream home and unlock the door to homeownership.

Determining a Fair Offer Price

One of the most crucial steps in home buying is determining a fair offer price. As a first-time home buyer, it's essential to understand how to evaluate a property's value to ensure you're making a sound investment. Here are a few key factors to consider when determining a fair offer price for your dream home.

Firstly, conducting thorough market research is vital. Look at recently sold properties in the same neighbourhood to understand the average sale price. Consider the homes' size, condition, and location to see how they compare to the property you're interested in. Online real estate platforms and local property listings can provide valuable data to guide decision-making.

Additionally, collaborating with a trusted real estate agent is highly recommended. They have extensive knowledge of the local market and can help you assess comparable sales, current market conditions, and any unique aspects of the property that may affect its value. Their expertise will prove invaluable when determining a fair offer price.

Another crucial component is getting a professional appraisal. An appraiser will evaluate the property's condition, size, location, and other relevant factors to provide an unbiased estimate of its value. This appraisal can serve as a reliable benchmark when determining your offer price. Although it comes with a cost, a professional appraisal ensures you're not overpaying for your dream home.

Consider the seller's motivation when determining your offer price. If the property has been on the market for an extended period, the seller may be more willing to negotiate. Similarly, if the seller needs to move quickly, they might be more open to accepting a lower offer. Understanding the seller's circumstances can give you an advantage when negotiating a fair price.

Lastly, it's essential to have a clear budget in mind. Determine what you can comfortably afford and consider any additional costs associated with home buying, such as closing costs, insurance, and maintenance. By having a well-defined budget, you can ensure that the offer you make aligns with your financial capacity.

Determining a fair offer price requires careful consideration of various factors, including market research, professional appraisals, collaboration with a real estate agent, and understanding the seller's motivation. By approaching this process thoughtfully, you can make an informed decision and secure your dream home at a fair price.

Negotiating with Sellers and Counteroffers

When purchasing your dream home, negotiating with sellers and handling counteroffers can be crucial to home-buying. Being well-prepared and knowledgeable ensures you get the best deal possible as a first-time buyer. This subchapter will discuss tips and strategies to help you navigate this stage successfully.

First and foremost, it's essential to do your homework and research the current market conditions. Understanding the local real estate market will give you an advantage when negotiating with sellers, as you will know the fair market value of the property you are interested in. This knowledge will help you make reasonable offers and avoid overpaying.

Once you have found a property you want, it's time to make an offer. Your initial offer should be well-thought-out and based on your budget, the property's value, and any necessary repairs or upgrades. It's essential to be realistic and avoid lowballing the seller, which may lead to a rejected offer or a negative impression.

After submitting your offer, it's common to receive a counteroffer from the seller. This is where negotiation skills come into play. Carefully review the counteroffer and consult your real estate agent or attorney to ensure you understand all the terms and conditions. You can then respond with a counter-counteroffer, aiming for a middle ground that satisfies both parties.

During negotiations, it's crucial to remain calm and patient. Remember that you and the seller want to reach an agreement, so finding common ground is the key. Be willing to compromise on non-essential items while firming on the most critical elements.

Another important aspect of negotiating with sellers is conducting thorough inspections. You can request repairs or renegotiate the purchase price if issues arise during the check. This step is vital to protect your investment and ensure you are not buying a property with hidden problems.

In conclusion, negotiating with sellers and handling counteroffers is essential to home-buying. As a first-time buyer, being well-prepared, knowledgeable about the market, and skilled in negotiation is crucial. By following these tips and strategies, you can increase your chances of securing your dream home at a price that suits your budget and needs.

Chapter 7

Conducting Inspections and Due Diligence

Hiring a Home Inspector

When purchasing your first home, it is crucial to thoroughly understand the property's condition before making a final decision. This is where a professional home inspector comes into play. Hiring a home inspector is essential in home-buying, as they can provide valuable insights and peace of mind.

A home inspector is a trained professional who examines the condition of a property, identifying any potential issues or areas of concern. They evaluate the structural integrity, electrical and plumbing systems, roofing, insulation, and more. By hiring an experienced home inspector, you can ensure that you are fully aware of any existing or potential problems within the property.

So, how do you find a reliable and qualified home inspector? Begin by asking for recommendations from friends, family, or real estate agents. They may have previously worked with a reputable inspector and can provide valuable insights. Additionally, online directories and professional associations, such as the American Society of Home Inspectors, can help you locate certified inspectors.

When interviewing potential home inspectors, ask about their experience, certifications, and if they carry professional liability insurance. A skilled inspector should be able to provide you with a sample inspection report to give you an idea of their thoroughness and attention to detail.

It is also essential to be present during the inspection process. This allows you to ask questions and better understand the inspector's findings. A good home inspector will identify issues and educate you on maintenance tips and potential future concerns.

Once the inspection is complete, you will receive a detailed report outlining the inspector's findings. This report will help you negotiate repairs or request a price reduction from the seller if necessary. Remember, the purpose of the inspection is not to find a flawless home but to ensure you are making an informed decision.

Remember that hiring a home inspector is an investment in your future. While an inspection may seem like an additional expense, it can save you from costly repairs. A thorough examination can give you peace of mind and confidence in purchasing your dream home.

In conclusion, hiring a home inspector is a crucial step in the home-buying process. Doing thorough research, interviewing potential inspectors, and being present during the inspection ensures that you are making an informed decision. Remember, a home inspector's role is to identify any existing or potential issues, allowing you to negotiate repairs or adjust your offer accordingly. Investing in a home inspection is a small price for the peace of mind it provides and the potential savings it can bring.

Evaluating Inspection Reports

Congratulations on embarking on the journey of purchasing your dream home! As a first-time homebuyer, you must equip yourself with the necessary knowledge to make informed decisions. One of the most vital steps in this process is evaluating inspection reports. This subchapter will guide you through the essential aspects to consider when reviewing these reports, ensuring you comprehensively understand your potential new home.

A professional home inspector thoroughly examines the property for structural, mechanical, or safety issues and prepares an inspection report. These reports provide valuable insights into the house's condition, identifying minor and major defects. When evaluating an inspection report, pay close attention to the following key areas:

1. Structural Integrity: Assess the overall stability and durability of the property. Look for cracks in the foundation, walls, or ceilings, as they may indicate structural problems that could be costly to repair.

2. Electrical and Plumbing Systems: Inspect the electrical and plumbing systems thoroughly. Ensure that they meet safety standards and are in good working condition. Faulty wiring or plumbing issues can lead to significant complications and expenses down the line.

3. Roof and Exterior: Examine the roof for any signs of leaks, missing shingles, or damaged flashing. Additionally, scrutinise the exterior walls, windows, and doors for potential water damage, rot, or pest infestations.

4. HVAC Systems: Evaluate the heating, ventilation, and air conditioning (HVAC) systems. These are critical for comfort and can be expensive to repair or replace. Confirm that they are in proper working order and have been adequately maintained.

5. Environmental Concerns: Inquire about potential environmental hazards such as asbestos, lead paint, or mould. These can pose health risks and may require professional remediation.

6. Safety Measures: Check for smoke detectors, carbon monoxide detectors, and fire extinguishers. Ensuring the property meets safety regulations is crucial for your and your family's well-being.

Remember that no home is perfect, and inspection reports often highlight issues that can be addressed with negotiation or repairs. Use the information from the inspection report to determine which items are deal-breakers and which can be resolved through negotiations with the seller.

You can decide whether to proceed with the purchase, renegotiate the terms, or walk away by carefully evaluating inspection reports. Working with a knowledgeable real estate agent and seeking professional advice can further enhance your understanding of the report and help you navigate this critical stage of the home-buying process.

Researching Property History and Disclosures

When buying your first home, gathering as much information as possible about the property you are interested in is crucial. Researching the property's history and disclosures is an essential step in the home-buying process, ensuring that you clearly understand the property's past and any potential issues it may have.

One of the first things you should do is research the property's history. This involves diving into public records, such as county and local government archives, to uncover details about the property's ownership, boundaries, and previous disputes or legal issues. Doing so lets you gain valuable insights into the property's background and identify potential red flags.

Additionally, it's essential to review the property's disclosures. The seller is obligated to disclose any known issues or defects that could affect the value or desirability of the property. These disclosures typically cover structural problems, water damage, pest infestations, or any history of renovations or repairs.

To obtain these disclosures, you can request them from the seller or the seller's agent. Carefully review the disclosures and ask any questions you may have. If something seems unclear or raises concerns, consider seeking advice from a professional, such as a home inspector or real estate attorney.

Furthermore, it's essential to conduct a thorough inspection of the property. While the seller's disclosures can provide valuable information, they may not reveal every potential issue. Hiring a qualified home inspector to assess the property can help uncover hidden problems, such as faulty electrical wiring, plumbing issues, or structural deficiencies. This inspection can save you from unexpected and costly repairs down the line.

Another valuable source of information is the neighbours. Contact them and inquire about the property's history, ongoing issues, or the neighbourhood. Neighbours can provide valuable insights not found in official records or disclosures.

In conclusion, researching the property's history and disclosures is crucial for first-time home buyers. By gathering as much information as possible, you can make an informed decision and avoid potential pitfalls. Remember to review the property's history, carefully examine the seller's disclosures, conduct a thorough inspection, and seek input from neighbours. You can unlock the door to your dream home with confidence and peace of mind.

Chapter 8

Completing the Purchase and Closing the Deal

Reviewing and Understanding Purchase Agreements

Congratulations! You have found your dream home and are ready to take the next step towards becoming a homeowner. However, before you can officially call it yours, there is an important document you need to review and understand – the purchase agreement. This subchapter will guide first-time homebuyers through reviewing and understanding purchase agreements, ensuring a smooth and informed decision-making process.

A purchase agreement is a legally binding document that outlines the terms and conditions of the sale between the buyer and the seller. It covers crucial aspects such as the purchase price, payment terms, contingencies, and closing date. As a first-time home buyer, it is essential to carefully review and comprehend this agreement to protect your interests and ensure a successful transaction.

When reviewing a purchase agreement, please read it thoroughly from beginning to end. Pay close attention to the purchase price and any contingencies listed. Contingencies are conditions that must be met for the sale, such as financing or a satisfactory home inspection. Ensure you understand the timeline for completing these contingencies and the consequences if they are not met.

Another vital aspect of the purchase agreement is the closing date. This is the day when ownership of the property officially transfers to you. Ensure the closing date aligns with your schedule and allows ample time for necessary preparations, such as obtaining financing or scheduling a final walkthrough.

It is also crucial to review any additional provisions or disclosures included in the agreement. These may include information about the property's condition, any known defects, or warranties provided by the seller. Ensure you understand the implications of these provisions and seek clarification if needed.

Once you have reviewed the purchase agreement, consulting with a real estate attorney or a knowledgeable professional is a good idea to ensure you fully understand the terms and conditions. They can provide valuable insights, answer questions, and offer guidance.

Remember, a purchase agreement is legally binding, and it is essential to review and understand it thoroughly before signing. Familiarising yourself with the terms and conditions will help you make an informed decision and protect your interests as a first-time home buyer.

In conclusion, reviewing and understanding purchase agreements is crucial for first-time home buyers. By carefully reviewing the terms and conditions, consulting with professionals, and seeking clarification when necessary, you can confidently navigate this process and ensure a successful home purchase.

Finalising Mortgage Details and Loan Approval

Buying your first home can be exciting but overwhelming, especially when finalising mortgage details and securing loan approval.

This subchapter aims to guide first-time home buyers through this crucial stage and provide them with the knowledge and tools they need to navigate this process successfully.

When you reach this stage, it's essential to understand the mortgage terms and conditions clearly. Take the time to review the terms thoroughly, including the interest rate, loan duration, and any additional fees or charges. If you have any questions or concerns, don't hesitate to contact your mortgage lender or a financial advisor who can provide guidance.

Before finalising the mortgage details, it's crucial to ensure that you have a strong credit score. Lenders will assess your creditworthiness before approving your loan, so keeping your credit in good shape is essential. Pay off any outstanding debts, ensure your credit card balances are low, and avoid taking on any new loans or credit cards during this time.

Loan approval is contingent on providing the necessary documentation to your lender. This typically includes proof of income, bank statements, tax returns, and employment verification. It's essential to gather these documents in advance and have them readily available to expedite the loan approval process.

As a first-time home buyer, you may qualify for various government programs or grants that can assist you in financing your home purchase. Research and explore these options to see if you meet the criteria and use any available financial support.

In addition to the mortgage details and loan approval process, it's also crucial to understand the concept of closing costs. These costs include fees associated with the home purchase, such as appraisal fees, title insurance, and attorney fees. Make sure to budget for these expenses and factor them into your overall financial plan.

Finally, never hesitate to seek professional guidance throughout this process. Working with a real estate agent, mortgage broker, or financial advisor can provide valuable insights and assistance in navigating the complexities of finalising mortgage details and loan approval.

First-time home buyers can ensure a smooth journey toward their dream home by understanding the mortgage terms, maintaining a good credit score, providing necessary documentation, exploring government programs, budgeting for closing costs, and seeking professional guidance. Remember, the key to unlocking the door to your dream home lies in your preparation and knowledge.

Attending the Closing Meeting and Signing Documents

Congratulations! You have finally reached the closing stage of your home-buying journey. This is an exciting moment as it signifies the final steps towards unlocking the door to your dream home. This subchapter will guide you through attending the closing meeting and signing the necessary documents.

The closing meeting is a vital step where you will meet with various parties involved in the transaction, such as your real estate agent, the seller's agent, the title company representative, and possibly an attorney. The purpose of this meeting is to review and sign all the legal documents required to transfer ownership of the property to you.

One of the critical documents you will encounter is the HUD-1 Settlement

Statement. This document outlines all the costs and fees associated with the purchase, such as the down payment, loan origination fees, property taxes, and title insurance. It is crucial to carefully review this statement to ensure accuracy and raise any questions or concerns you may have.

Another significant document is the promissory note, which details the terms and conditions of your mortgage loan. Understand the interest rate, repayment schedule, and any penalties for late payments. Take your time to read through this document thoroughly, as it will help you understand your financial obligations.

During the closing meeting, you must also sign the deed, which transfers property ownership to your name. This legal document is crucial, and you should ensure that your name is spelt correctly and matches the information provided on your loan application.

In addition to signing documents, you must provide certified funds or arrange wire transfers to cover the closing costs and down payment. Ensure you have the necessary funds to avoid delays or complications during the closing process.

Attending the closing meeting can be overwhelming, but remember you are not alone. Your real estate agent or attorney will be there to guide you and answer any questions you may have. Take your time to review each document and seek clarification if needed. Once everything is signed and the funds are transferred, you will finally be the proud owner of your dream home.

In conclusion, attending the closing meeting and signing the necessary documents is the final step in becoming a homeowner. It is essential to be well-prepared, review all the papers thoroughly, and ask questions to ensure a smooth and successful closing. Congratulations on reaching this milestone, and get ready to unlock the door to your dream home!

Chapter 9

Moving In and Settling Down

Organising and Planning for a Smooth Move

Congratulations! You've finally found your dream home and are ready to leap into homeownership. Now comes the exciting yet daunting task of planning and organising your move. This chapter will guide you through the essential steps to ensure a smooth and stress-free transition into your new home.

The first step in organising your move is to create a comprehensive checklist. This will help you stay organised and avoid overlooking any critical details. Start by listing all the tasks you must complete, such as notifying utility providers, hiring a moving company, and packing your belongings. Break down these tasks into smaller steps to make the process more manageable.

Next, it's time to declutter and downsize. Moving provides the perfect opportunity to rid yourself of unnecessary items that have accumulated over the years. Sort your belongings and decide what to keep, donate, or sell. Not only will this help streamline your move, but it will also make your new home feel more organised and clutter-free.

Once you have downsized, it's time to start packing. Begin by acquiring the necessary packing supplies, such as boxes, bubble wrap, and packing tape. Pack room by room, labelling each box with its contents and destination within your new home. This will simplify the unpacking process and save time searching for specific items.

In addition to packing, don't forget to update your address with the postal service, banks, insurance providers, and any other institutions that need to know your new location. This will ensure your mail and important documents are forwarded to the correct address.

Make sure to have a plan on the day of the move. Communicate with your moving company or friends to coordinate logistics and ensure everyone is on the same page. Take the time to do a final walkthrough of your old home, ensuring nothing has been left behind.

Finally, once you've arrived at your new home, take some time to settle in and get acclimated. Unpack your essentials, such as bedding, toiletries, and kitchen items. This will help you feel more comfortable in your new space while unpacking over the coming days or weeks.

These organising and planning tips will prepare you for a smooth and successful move into your dream home. Remember, while the process may seem overwhelming sometimes, the result will be worth it. Good luck, and enjoy the journey of homeownership!

Setting Up Utilities and Essential Services

Congratulations on taking the first step towards homeownership! As a first-time home buyer, there are several important tasks you need to tackle before settling into your dream home. One crucial aspect is setting up utilities and essential services, which ensure a smooth transition into your new abode. This subchapter will guide you through the process, providing valuable information and tips to make this task hassle-free.

Regarding utilities, you'll typically need to set up electricity, water, gas, and internet services. Start by contacting the local utility companies in your area to initiate the process. Doing this well in advance, preferably a week or two before your move-in date, is recommended to avoid inconveniences. Please list the necessary contact details and keep them handy during the transition.

Before setting up utilities, it's crucial to research and compare providers to secure the best rates and packages. You can find this information online, through local directories, or by seeking recommendations from friends and neighbours. By doing your due diligence, you can potentially save money in the long run.

Apart from utilities, other essential services need to be considered as well. These include garbage collection, recycling, and sewage services. Contact your local municipality or waste management companies to understand the process and obtain necessary information regarding schedules and fees.

Additionally, you may need to set up services like cable TV, landline phones (if desired), and security systems. Research different service providers in your area, compare packages and select the ones that suit your needs and budget. Remember to inquire about installation fees, contract terms, and any promotional offers available.

Creating a checklist of all the utilities and essential services you need to set up is advisable to ensure a smooth transition. Tick off each item as you complete it, ensuring nothing is forgotten or left until the last minute.

Setting up utilities and essential services is vital for moving into your dream home. By being proactive and taking the time to research and compare different providers, you can ensure that you secure the best deals and packages. This will save you money and make your transition into your new home stress-free and enjoyable.

Remember, as a first-time home buyer, it's normal to sometimes feel overwhelmed. However, by following this subchapter's guidelines and taking things step by step, you'll be well on your way to unlocking the door to your dream home.

Making Your New House Feel Like Home

Congratulations on becoming a first-time home buyer! Owning your dream home is an exciting milestone, and now it's time to transform your house into a place that truly feels like home. In this subchapter, we will explore some helpful tips and tricks to help you settle into your new abode and create a warm and inviting atmosphere.

1.   Personalise Your Space: Add your personal touch to each room. Hang family photos, display treasured keepsakes, or incorporate artwork that resonates with your style and personality. Surrounding yourself with familiar items instantly makes your new house feel like home.

2. Unpack with Purpose: Unpacking can be daunting, but strategically doing it will make a big difference. Begin with the essentials, such as kitchenware and bedroom items, to ensure daily routines resume smoothly. As you progress, take the time to declutter and organise each room, creating a sense of order and tranquillity.

3. Create Cozy Nooks: Identify areas where you can create cosy nooks for relaxation or hobbies in your new home. Whether it's a reading corner with a comfortable chair and soft lighting or a crafting space with ample storage, having designated areas for activities you enjoy will make your house more personalised and inviting.

4. Add Greenery: Bring nature indoors by incorporating plants and flowers into your living spaces. Indoor plants provide aesthetic appeal, purify the air, and improve overall well-being. Choose easy-to-maintain varieties if you're new to gardening, and gradually expand your collection as you become more confident.

5. Host a Housewarming Party: Invite your friends, family, and new neighbours to celebrate your new home. Hosting a housewarming party establishes connections and helps you create memories within your space. It's an opportunity to showcase your house, receive warm wishes, and build community.

6. Embrace Rituals: Establishing rituals can make your new house feel like home in no time. Whether it's a Sunday movie night, a weekly family dinner, or morning yoga sessions, incorporating regular activities will help create a comforting routine and foster a sense of belonging.

Remember, turning a house into a home is a gradual process. It takes time to settle in and find the perfect balance that reflects your unique style and preferences. By incorporating these tips, you'll be well on your way to transforming your new house into a place where you feel truly at home. Enjoy the journey!

Chapter 10

Maintaining and Protecting Your Investment

Creating a Home Maintenance Schedule

Being a first-time homebuyer is an exciting milestone but comes with many responsibilities. One crucial aspect of homeownership is maintaining your dream home to ensure its longevity and value. This subchapter will guide you through creating a home maintenance schedule, helping you stay organised and proactive in caring for your new property.

As a first-time homeowner, it's important to understand that regular maintenance is essential to prevent minor issues from becoming major problems. Developing a maintenance schedule lets you stay on top of tasks and catch potential issues before they escalate.

Firstly, it's essential to identify the key areas that require regular attention. These may include the HVAC, plumbing, electrical, roof, gutters, windows, and landscaping.

Each component of your home has unique maintenance needs, and it's essential to understand and address them accordingly.

Next, determine the frequency of maintenance tasks for each area. Some duties, such as changing air filters or cleaning gutters, may need to be performed monthly or quarterly, while others, like inspecting the roof or servicing the HVAC system, may be done annually. You can ensure nothing is overlooked by breaking down tasks into a schedule.

Consider using a digital or physical calendar to track your maintenance schedule to stay organised. Set reminders for specific tasks and allocate time in your schedule to complete them. Additionally, it can be helpful to create a checklist for each mission, outlining the necessary steps to ensure nothing is missed.

Remember to prioritise safety while performing maintenance tasks. If you're unsure about any aspect, it's best to consult professionals who specialise in the respective field. They can offer guidance, perform inspections, and provide necessary repairs or maintenance.

Lastly, maintaining a record of all maintenance activities is essential. Not only will this help you stay organised, but it will also be valuable information for potential future buyers. Keep receipts, warranties, and any documentation related to maintenance and repairs in a safe place.

Creating a home maintenance schedule is a proactive step toward safeguarding your investment and ensuring the long-term quality of your dream home. By staying organised, promptly addressing tasks, and seeking professional help, you can enjoy your new house for years.

Understanding Homeowners Insurance

As a first-time home buyer, one of the most critical aspects of your journey towards homeownership is understanding homeowners insurance. This crucial protection provides financial security and peace of mind, shielding you from unforeseen events that could damage or destroy your dream home.

Homeowners insurance is a contract between you and an insurance company that safeguards your property and possessions from natural disasters, theft, and liability claims. It is essential to comprehend the different aspects of this insurance to ensure you have the right coverage for your needs.

First and foremost, it's essential to understand the various types of coverage homeowners insurance offers. The most common form is called dwelling coverage, which protects the structure of your home and any attached structures, such as a garage or deck. This coverage typically extends to damages caused by fire, windstorms, hail, lightning, and other specified perils.

Additionally, homeowners insurance includes personal property coverage, which safeguards your belongings, such as furniture, electronics, and clothing, in case of theft, vandalism, or covered perils. It's crucial to accurately assess the value of your possessions to ensure you have sufficient coverage.

Liability coverage is another vital component of homeowners insurance. This protects you from legal and financial responsibility if someone gets injured on your property and decides to file a lawsuit. Liability coverage also extends to damages caused by you or your family members to others' property.

Understanding the concept of deductibles is equally essential for homeowners insurance. A deductible is paid out of pocket before your insurance coverage kicks in. Choosing a deductible that aligns with your financial capabilities is crucial, as a higher deductible will lower your premium but increase your upfront costs in the event of a claim.

Lastly, reviewing the exclusions and limitations of your homeowner's insurance policy is essential. Some policies might not cover specific perils, such as floods or earthquakes, which require separate coverage. Understanding these exclusions is vital to protect yourself adequately.

In conclusion, understanding homeowners insurance is crucial for first-time home buyers. It provides financial security and peace of mind, protecting your dream home from unforeseen events. By comprehending the various coverage options, deductibles, and exclusions, you can ensure you have the proper homeowner's insurance policy to safeguard your investment and belongings.

Dealing with Repairs and Renovations

One of the most exciting aspects of owning a home is the opportunity to personalise and improve it to suit your needs and preferences. However, repairs and renovations can be daunting for first-time home buyers. This subchapter will explore some essential tips and guidelines to help you navigate this process smoothly and efficiently.

First and foremost, it is crucial to prioritise repairs and renovations based on their urgency and significance. Start by identifying any immediate issues that require attention, such as leaky faucets, faulty electrical wiring, or structural problems. These repairs should take precedence to ensure the safety and functionality of your new home.

Once the necessary repairs are addressed, you can move on to renovations to enhance your living space. Establishing a realistic budget and sticking to it throughout the renovation process is essential. Research the average costs of different projects in your area and consult with professionals for accurate estimates. This will help you avoid overspending and ensure you get the best value for your money.

Before embarking on any renovation project, take the time to research and plan thoroughly. Create a detailed timeline, outline your goals, and consider consulting with an interior designer or contractor for expert advice. They can help you maximise your space and suggest cost-effective solutions that align with your vision.

When hiring professionals for repairs or renovations, it is crucial to do your due diligence. Seek recommendations from friends, family, and colleagues, and always ask for references before making a final decision. Don't be afraid to interview multiple contractors and request detailed quotes to compare prices and services. Remember, quality artistry is worth the investment in the long run.

Lastly, always expect the unexpected. Renovations can be unpredictable, and preparing for unforeseen challenges is vital. Set aside a contingency fund to account for any incidental expenses or delays. Flexibility and patience are essential when dealing with repairs and renovations, as they often take longer or cost more than anticipated.

Following these guidelines, you can confidently approach repairs and renovations and turn your new house into your dream home. Remember, it is a journey, and with proper planning and organisation, you can

overcome any obstacles and create a space
that reflects your unique style and
personality.

Chapter 11

Advancing Your Homeownership Journey

Building Equity and Considering Investment Opportunities

As a first-time home buyer, purchasing your dream home is an exciting and significant milestone. However, it is essential to consider the long-term financial benefits and potential investment opportunities that come with homeownership. In this subchapter, we will explore the concept of building equity and how it can open doors to future financial growth.

Building equity is one of the primary advantages of owning a home. Equity refers to the difference between the market value of your property and the outstanding balance on your mortgage. Over time, as you make mortgage payments and the value of your home appreciates your equity increases. This equity can be a valuable asset that can be utilised for various purposes, such as financing home improvements, paying off debts, or even purchasing additional properties.

One way to build equity is by making regular mortgage payments. Each payment reduces the principal amount owed and increases your ownership stake in the property. Additionally, making extra payments or increasing your monthly instalment can accelerate building equity. It is important to note that building equity is a long-term commitment, and patience is vital. However, the rewards can be significant, providing you with a solid financial foundation for the future.

Considering investment opportunities is another crucial aspect of homeownership. Real estate has historically proven a sound investment choice, with properties appreciating over time. As a first-time buyer, your home can serve as an investment vehicle that offers potential returns in the future. By carefully selecting a property in a desirable location with growth potential, you can maximise your investment and potentially profit from it when you decide to sell.

Furthermore, owning a home opens up opportunities for passive income generation. Renting out a portion of your property, such as a basement or an extra room, can provide a steady income stream. This additional income can help cover monthly expenses or contribute towards paying off your mortgage faster.

In conclusion, building equity and considering investment opportunities are vital components of homeownership. By making regular mortgage payments and taking advantage of the potential returns in the real estate market, you can secure your financial future and unlock the doors to further investment opportunities. Homeownership is about finding your dream home and building a solid foundation for economic growth and prosperity.

Refinancing and Mortgage Options

When purchasing your dream home, financing is one of the most critical aspects. As a first-time home buyer, understanding the concept of refinancing and the various mortgage options available will significantly aid you in making informed decisions. In this subchapter, we will delve into the world of refinancing and explore different mortgage options, providing you with the knowledge necessary to unlock the door to your dream home.

Refinancing is essentially the process of replacing an existing mortgage with a new one that offers better terms. It can benefit homeowners who want to lower their monthly payments, reduce the interest rate, or change the loan term. Refinancing can save thousands of dollars on your mortgage or gain access to equity for other financial needs.

Before considering refinancing, evaluating your financial situation and goals is crucial. Depending on your circumstances, you may opt for a rate-and-term refinance, which allows you to secure a lower interest rate or change the loan term. Alternatively, a cash-out refinance may be suitable if you need to access the equity in your home for renovations, debt consolidation, or other significant expenses.

Understanding your various mortgage options is equally important in your home-buying journey. The most common types of mortgages include fixed-rate mortgages, adjustable-rate mortgages (ARMs), and government-backed loans such as FHA and VA loans.

Fixed-rate mortgages provide stability and peace of mind as the interest rate remains constant throughout the loan term. On the other hand, ARMs offer lower initial rates that adjust periodically based on market conditions. Government-backed loans are designed to assist first-time home buyers who may have limited funds for a down payment or have specific eligibility requirements.

As a first-time home buyer, it is crucial to explore the options offered by different lenders and compare their terms, interest rates, and fees. Additionally, seeking professional guidance from a mortgage broker or financial advisor can help you navigate the complex landscape of refinancing and mortgage options, ensuring you make the best decision for your unique situation.

In conclusion, refinancing and mortgage options play a vital role in the home-buying process. By understanding the concept of refinancing and exploring various mortgage options available, you can make well-informed decisions that align with your financial goals. Remember to evaluate your financial situation, explore different lenders, and seek expert advice to maximise your chances of unlocking the door to your dream home.

Tips for Upsizing or Downsizing in the Future

As a first-time home buyer, it's essential to consider your current needs and plans. Whether you envision expanding your family or scaling down for a simpler lifestyle, the decision to upsize or downsize your home can significantly impact your finances and overall happiness. This subchapter will provide valuable tips to help you navigate the process of upsizing or downsizing in the future.

1. Plan: When purchasing your first home, thinking long-term is essential. Consider your future needs and aspirations. Will you need more space for a growing family or desire a smaller, low-maintenance property in retirement? By understanding your goals, you can make a more informed decision when to upsize or downsize.

2. Financial implications: Upsizing or downsizing can have financial consequences. Upsizing typically means a larger mortgage, increased maintenance costs, and potentially higher property taxes. Conversely, downsizing may free up equity, reduce expenses, and lower property taxes. Be sure to carefully evaluate your financial situation

and consult a financial advisor before making any decisions.

3. Location considerations: When upsizing or downsizing, it's essential to consider the location of your new home. Research neighbourhoods and amenities that align with your lifestyle and plans. If you have children or plan to start a family, proximity to good schools and parks may be crucial. Conversely, if you're downsizing for retirement, you may prioritise accessibility to healthcare facilities and recreational activities.

4. Storage needs: Both upsizing and downsizing can present storage challenges. If you're upsizing, consider whether the property offers sufficient storage space for your belongings. Downsizing requires carefully considering what items are essential and what can be sold, donated, or stored. It's important to declutter and organise your possessions to maximise space in a smaller home.

5. Emotional attachment: Moving is not just a physical process; it's an emotional one too. Upsizing or downsizing can bring a mix of emotions, especially if you have sentimental attachments to your current home. Take time

to acknowledge and channel these emotions positively. Please focus on the exciting possibilities in your new house, whether it's a bigger space for new memories or a smaller, more manageable living arrangement.

By following these tips and considering your plans, you can make a well-informed decision regarding upsizing or downsizing your home. Remember, your dream home may evolve, and adapting to your changing needs and circumstances is crucial.

Chapter 12

Embracing the Joys of Homeownership

Building a Sense of Community

Building a sense of community is one of the most critical aspects of finding and creating your dream home. As a first-time homebuyer, it's essential to understand the significance of this, as it can significantly enhance your overall lifestyle and happiness in your new neighbourhood. This subchapter will explore how to foster a strong sense of community and why it matters.

When searching for your dream home, consider the neighbourhood's characteristics beyond the property. Look for areas that promote a community-focused lifestyle, such as parks, community centres, or local businesses. These features often indicate a tight-knit community that values relationships and engagement. Additionally, research the neighbourhood's history, events, and local organisations to gain insight into the community's culture and potential for you to fit in.

Once you've moved into your new home, take proactive steps to connect with your neighbours. Introduce yourself with a friendly smile and a warm handshake, and be open to community events or gatherings invitations. Participate in local activities, such as volunteering, joining clubs or sports teams, or attending neighbourhood meetings. These actions will help you establish relationships and build a network of friends with similar interests.

Another way to build community is by organising events or social gatherings in your home. Host a neighbourhood potluck, game night, or block party to unite people and foster a sense of belonging. Encourage your neighbours to participate by distributing invitations, creating a Facebook group, or posting flyers in common areas. These events will help you get to know your neighbours better and create a welcoming atmosphere for newcomers.

Additionally, consider joining online platforms or social media groups specific to your neighbourhood. These platforms often serve as a virtual gathering place where residents can share information, ask for recommendations, or organise community initiatives. By actively participating in these online communities, you can stay updated on local news, connect with like-minded individuals, and contribute to building a stronger sense of community.

In conclusion, building a sense of community is vital when purchasing your first home. It enhances your overall living experience, creates a support system, and fosters a sense of belonging. By actively engaging with your neighbours, participating in local activities, hosting events, and utilising online platforms, you can unlock the door to a vibrant and inclusive community that will make your dream home come alive.

Personalising Your Space

One of the most exciting aspects of buying your first home is the opportunity to personalise and make it your own. Your new home is a blank canvas waiting to be filled with your unique style and personality. This subchapter will explore tips and ideas to help you personalise your space and create a home that reflects your taste and preferences.

1. Define your style: Before diving into decorating, take some time to identify your style. Are you drawn to a more traditional look or prefer a modern, minimalist aesthetic? Understanding your style will guide your choices and ensure a cohesive and harmonious design throughout your home.

2. Start with the basics: Select a colour scheme that resonates with you. Colours significantly impact our mood and can set the tone for a room. Experiment with different shades and combinations to find the perfect palette for each space in your home.

3. Furniture and accessories: Carefully choose pieces that suit your style and meet your functional needs. Consider the layout of each room and the flow of traffic. Don't forget to add personal touches with accessories, such as artwork, family photographs, and decorative items that hold sentimental value.

4. DIY projects: Personalising your space doesn't have to break the bank. Engage in do-it-yourself projects to add a personal touch to your home. From repurposing old furniture to creating custom artwork, there are endless possibilities to showcase your creativity.

5. Embrace nature: Incorporating natural elements into your home can bring a sense of calm and tranquillity. Add indoor plants, fresh flowers, or even a small herb garden to connect with nature and create a refreshing atmosphere.

6. Lighting matters: Good lighting can make a difference in any space. Experiment with different lighting fixtures and styles to create the desired ambience. From statement chandeliers to soft accent lighting, choose options that enhance the mood of each room.

7. Flexibility for change: Remember that personalisation is an ongoing process. As your tastes and preferences evolve, so should your home. Invest in versatile furniture and decor that can be easily updated or rearranged to accommodate your changing needs.

Personalising your space is about creating a home that brings you joy and reflects your unique personality. Take the time to explore different styles, experiment with colours, and have fun designing your dream home. Happy decorating!

Celebrating Milestones and Creating Memories

As a first-time homebuyer, stepping into the world of real estate can feel overwhelming. From searching for the perfect property to navigating the financial aspects, the journey to homeownership is filled with excitement and challenges. However, beyond the practicalities, it's essential to remember that buying a home is not just a transaction; it's a milestone worth celebrating and a chance to create lifelong memories.

Owning your dream home is a significant achievement, and taking a moment to acknowledge and embrace this milestone is crucial. After all, your efforts to save, plan, and find your perfect abode deserve recognition. Whether throwing a housewarming party, inviting friends and family to share in your joy, or simply indulging in a quiet celebration, take the time to revel in your accomplishment.

Beyond the initial celebration, your dream home also becomes the canvas for countless memories that will shape your life. Every step you take within those four walls will become part of your personal story from the moment you turn the key for the first time.

The laughter shared during family gatherings, the aroma of home-cooked meals wafting through the kitchen, and the comfort of snuggling up on the couch for movie nights are the memories that will make your house a home.

Creating memories in your dream home extends beyond its walls. Take advantage of the surrounding neighbourhood and community to build a fulfilling life. Explore local parks, join community events, and get to know your neighbours. These experiences will enhance your homeownership journey and help you feel connected to your new surroundings.

Documenting your milestones can be an excellent way to cherish and reflect on your journey. Consider starting a home journal to journal significant events, milestones, and memories. From the first renovation project to the growth of your family, capturing these moments on paper will allow you to revisit and appreciate how far you've come.

Ultimately, celebrating milestones and creating memories in your dream home reminds you of the joy that homeownership can bring. Your first home is not just a financial investment; it's a sanctuary where dreams can unfold and memories can be made. So, as you embark on this exciting journey, remember to savour every step, celebrate your achievements, and embrace the infinite possibilities that await you within the walls of your dream home.